What's New in Java 8

An unofficial guide

Adam L. Davis

What's New in Java 8

An unofficial guide

Adam L. Davis

This book is for sale at http://leanpub.com/whatsnewinjava8

This version was published on 2014-05-06

ISBN 978-1497533509

Tweet This Book!

Please help Adam L. Davis by spreading the word about this book on Twitter!

The suggested hashtag for this book is #whatsnewinjava8.

Find out what other people are saying about the book by clicking on this link to search for this hashtag on Twitter:

https://twitter.com/search?q=#whatsnewinjava8

Also By Adam L. Davis

Modern Java

Modern Programming Made Easy

Contents

Preface

Like many Java developers, the first time I heard about lambda expressions it piqued my interest. Also like many others, I was disappointed when it was set back. However, it is better late than never.

Java 8 is a giant step forward for the Java language. Writing this book has forced me to learn a lot more about it. In Project Lambda, Java gets a new closure syntax, method-references, and default methods on interfaces. It manages to add many of the features of functional languages without losing the clarity and simplicity Java developers have come to expect.

Aside from Project Lambda, Java 8 also gets a new Date and Time API (JSR 310), the Nashorn JavaScript engine, and removes the Permanent Generation from the HotSpot virtual machine, among other changes.

I would like to acknowledge the following people for providing valuable resources:

- Brian Goetz – "State of the Lambda"[1]
- Aleksey Shipilev – jdk8-lambda-samples[2]
- Richard Warburton – "Java 8 Lambdas"[3]
- Julien Ponge – "Oracle Nashorn" in the Jan./Feb. 2014 issue of Java Magazine.
- Venkat Subramaniam – agiledeveloper.com[4]
- All of the developers behind Java 8.
- The developers of Guava, joda-time, Groovy, and Scala.

---

[1] http://cr.openjdk.java.net/~briangoetz/lambda/lambda-state-final.html

[2] https://github.com/shipilev/jdk8-lambda-samples

[3] http://shop.oreilly.com/product/0636920030713.do

[4] http://blog.agiledeveloper.com/

1 Overview

This book is a short introduction to Java 8. After reading it, you should have a basic understanding of the new features and be ready to start using it.

This book assumes that you have a good understanding of Java the language and the JVM. If you're not familiar with the language, including features of Java 7, it might be hard to follow some of the examples.

Java 8 includes the following:

- Lambda expressions
- Method references
- Default Methods (Defender methods)
- A new Stream API.
- Optional
- A new Date/Time API.
- Nashorn, the new JavaScript engine
- Removal of the Permanent Generation
- and more...

The best way to read this book is with a Java 8 supporting IDE running so you can try out the new features.

 Code examples can be found on github[1].

---

[1]https://github.com/adamd/hellojava8

2 Lambda Expressions

The biggest new feature of Java 8 is language level support for *lambda expressions* (Project Lambda). A lambda expression is like syntactic sugar for an anonymous class[1] with one method whose type is inferred. However, it will have enormous implications for simplifying development.

2.1 Syntax

The main syntax of a lambda expression is "parameters -> body". The compiler can usually use the context of the lambda expression to determine the functional interface[2] being used and the types of the parameters. There are four important rules to the syntax:

- Declaring the types of the parameters is optional.
- Using parentheses around the parameter is optional if you have only one parameter.
- Using curly braces is optional (unless you need multiple statements).
- The "return" keyword is optional if you have a single expression that returns a value.

Here are some examples of the syntax:

```
1  () -> System.out.println(this)
2  (String str) -> System.out.println(str)
3  str -> System.out.println(str)
4  (String s1, String s2) -> { return s2.length() - s1.length(); }
5  (s1, s2) -> s2.length() - s1.length()
```

The last expression could be used to sort a list; for example:

```
1  Arrays.sort(strArray,
2    (String s1, String s2) -> s2.length() - s1.length());
```

In this case the lambda expression implements the Comparator interface to sort strings by length.

2.2 Scope

Here's a short example of using lambdas with the Runnable interface:

---

[1] A lambda expression is *not* an anonymous class; it actually uses invokedynamic in the byte-code.

[2] We will explain what "functional interface" means in a later section.

```java
1   import static java.lang.System.out;
2
3   public class Hello {
4           Runnable r1 = () -> out.println(this);
5           Runnable r2 = () -> out.println(toString());
6
7           public String toString() { return "Hello, world!"; }
8
9           public static void main(String... args) {
10                  new Hello().r1.run(); //Hello, world!
11                  new Hello().r2.run(); //Hello, world!
12          }
13  }
```

The important thing to note is both the r1 and r2 lambdas call the toString() method of the Hello class. This demonstrates the scope available to the lambda.

You can also refer to final variables or *effectively* final variables. A variable is effectively final if it is only assigned once.

For example, using Spring's HibernateTemplate:

```java
1   String sql = "delete * from User";
2   getHibernateTemplate().execute(session ->
3       session.createSQLQuery(sql).uniqueResult());
```

In the above, you can refer to the variable sql because it is only assigned once. If you were to assign to it a second time, it would cause a compilation error.

2.3 Method references

Since a lambda expression is like an object-less method, wouldn't be nice if we could refer to existing methods instead of using a lamda expression? This is exactly what we can do with *method references*.

For example, imagine you frequently need to filter a list of Files based on file types. Assume you have the following set of methods for determining a file's type:

```
1  public class FileFilters {
2          public static boolean fileIsPdf(File file) {/*code*/}
3          public static boolean fileIsTxt(File file) {/*code*/}
4          public static boolean fileIsRtf(File file) {/*code*/}
5  }
```

Whenever you want to filter a list of files, you can use a method reference as in the following example (assuming you already defined a method getFiles() that returns a Stream):

```
1  Stream<File> pdfs = getFiles().filter(FileFilters::fileIsPdf);
2  Stream<File> txts = getFiles().filter(FileFilters::fileIsTxt);
3  Stream<File> rtfs = getFiles().filter(FileFilters::fileIsRtf);
```

Method references can point to:

- Static methods.
- Instance methods.
- Methods on *particular* instances.
- Constructors (ie. TreeSet::new)

For example, using the new java.nio.file.Files.lines method:

```
1  Files.lines(Paths.get("Nio.java"))
2              .map(String::trim)
3              .forEach(System.out::println);
```

The above reads the file "Nio.java", calls trim() on every line, and then prints out the lines.

Notice that System.out::println refers to the println method on an instance of PrintStream.

2.4 Functional Interfaces

In Java 8 a *functional interface* is defined as an interface with exactly one abstract method. This even applies to interfaces that were created with previous versions of Java.

Java 8 comes with several new functional interfaces in the package, java.util.function.

- Function<T,R> - takes an object of type T and returns R.
- Supplier<T> - just returns an object of type T.
- Predicate<T> - returns a boolean value based on input of type T.

- Consumer‹T› - performs an action with given object of type T.
- BiFunction - like Function but with two parameters.
- BiConsumer - like Consumer but with two parameters.

It also comes with several corresponding interfaces for primitive types, such as:

- IntConsumer
- IntFunction‹R›
- IntPredicate
- IntSupplier

 See the java.util.function Javadocs[3] for more information.

The coolest thing about functional interfaces is that they can be assigned to anything that would fulfill their contract. Take the following code for example:

```
1  Function<String, String> atr = (name) -> {return "@" + name;};
2  Function<String, Integer> leng = (name) -> name.length();
3  Function<String, Integer> leng2 = String::length;
```

This code is perfectly valid Java 8. The first line defines a function that prepends "@" to a String. The last two lines define functions that do the same thing: get the length of a String.

The Java compiler is smart enough to convert the method reference to String's length() method into a Function (a functional interface) whose apply method takes a String and returns an Integer. For example:

```
1  for (String s : args) out.println(leng2.apply(s));
```

This would print out the lengths of the given strings.

Any interface can be functional interface, not merely those that come with Java. To declare your intention that an interface is functional, use the @FunctionalInterface annotation. Although not necessary, it will cause a compilation error if your interface does not satisfy the requirements (ie. one abstract method).

 ## Github

See jdk8-lambda-samples[4] for more examples.

---

[3]http://download.java.net/jdk8/docs/api/java/util/function/package-summary.html
[4]https://github.com/katoquro/jdk8-lambda-samples

2.5 Comparisons to Java 7

To better illustrate the benefit of Lambda-expressions, here are some examples of how code from Java 7 can be shortened in Java 8.

Creating an ActionListener

```
1  // Java 7
2  ActionListener al = new ActionListener() {
3      @Override
4      public void actionPerformed(ActionEvent e) {
5          System.out.println(e.getActionCommand());
6      }
7  };
8  // Java 8
9  ActionListener al8 = e -> System.out.println(e.getActionCommand());
```

Printing out a list of Strings

```
1  // Java 7
2  for (String s : list) {
3      System.out.println(s);
4  }
5  //Java 8
6  list.forEach(System.out::println);
```

Sorting a list of Strings

```
1   // Java 7
2   Collections.sort(list, new Comparator<String>() {
3       @Override
4       public int compare(String s1, String s2) {
5           return s1.length() - s2.length();
6       }
7   });
8   //Java 8
9   Collections.sort(list, (s1, s2) -> s1.length() - s2.length());
10  // or
11  list.sort(Comparator.comparingInt(String::length));
```

Sorting

For the sorting examples, assume you have the following Person class:

```
1   public static class Person {
2
3       String firstName;
4       String lastName;
5
6       public String getFirstName() {
7           return firstName;
8       }
9
10      public String getLastName() {
11          return lastName;
12      }
13  }
```

Here's how you might sort this list in Java 7 by last-name and then first-name:

```
1   Collections.sort(list, new Comparator<Person>() {
2       @Override
3       public int compare(Person p1, Person p2) {
4           int n = p1.getLastName().compareTo(p2.getLastName());
5           if (n == 0) {
6               return p1.getFirstName().compareTo(p2.getFirstName());
7           }
8           return n;
9       }
10  });
```

In Java 8, this can be shortened to the following:

```
1   list.sort(Comparator.comparing(Person::getLastName)
2           .thenComparing(Person::getFirstName));
```

 This example uses a static method on an interface (comparing) and a default method (thenComparing) which are discussed in the next chapter.

3 Default Methods

In order to add the `stream` method (or any others) to the core Collections API, Java needed another new feature, *Default methods* (also known as *Defender Methods* or *Virtual Extension methods*). This way they could add new methods to the `List` interface for example without breaking all the existing implementations (backwards compatibility).

Default methods can be added to any interface. Like the name implies, any class that implements the interface but does not override the method will get the default implementation.

For example, the `stream` method in the `Collection` interface is defined something like the following:

```
1  default public Stream stream() {
2          return StreamSupport.stream(spliterator());
3  }
```

 See the Java docs[1] for more on Spliterators.

You can always override a default method if you need different behavior.

3.1 Default and Functional

An interface can have one or more default methods and still be functional.

For example, take a look at the Iterable interface:

```
1   @FunctionalInterface
2   public interface Iterable {
3           Iterator iterator();
4           default void forEach(Consumer<? super T> action) {
5                   Objects.requireNonNull(action);
6                   for (T t : this) {
7                           action.accept(t);
8                   }
9           }
10  }
```

It has both the `iterator()` method and the `forEach` method.

---

[1]http://download.java.net/jdk8/docs/api/java/util/Collection.html#spliterator--

3.2 Multiple Defaults

In the unlikely case that your class implements two or more interfaces that define the same default method, Java will throw a compilation error. You will need to override the method and choose from one of the methods. For example:

```
1  interface Foo {
2          default void talk() {
3                  out.println("Foo!");
4          }
5  }
6  interface Bar {
7          default void talk() {
8                  out.println("Bar!");
9          }
10 }
11 class FooBar implements Foo, Bar {
12         @Override
13         void talk() { Foo.super.talk(); }
14 }
```

In the above code, `talk` is overridden and calls `Foo`'s talk method. This is similar to the way you refer to a super class in pre-Java-8.

3.3 Static Methods on Interface

Although not strictly related to default methods, the ability to add static methods to interfaces is a similar change to the Java language.

For example, there are many static methods on the new *Stream* interface. This makes "helper" methods easier to find since they can be located directly on the interface, instead of a different class such as *StreamUtil* or *Streams*.

Here's an example in the new *Stream* interface:

```
1  public static<T> Stream<T> of(T... values) {
2      return Arrays.stream(values);
3  }
```

The above method creates a new stream based on the given values.

4 Streams

The Stream interface is such a fundamental part of Java 8 it deserves its own chapter.

4.1 What is a Stream?

The Stream interface is located in the java.util.stream package. It represents a sequence of objects somewhat like the Iterator interface. However, unlike the Iterator, it supports parallel execution.

The Stream interface supports the map/filter/reduce pattern and executes lazily, forming the basis (along with lambdas) for functional-style programming in Java 8.

There are also corresponding primitive streams (IntStream, DoubleStream, and LongStream) for performance reasons.

4.2 Generating Streams

There are many ways to create a Stream in Java 8. Many of the existing Java core library classes have Stream returning methods in Java 8.

Streaming Collections

The most obvious way to create a stream is from a Collection.

The Collection interface has two default methods on it for creating streams:

- stream(): Returns a sequential Stream with the collection as its source.
- parallelStream(): Returns a possibly parallel Stream with the collection as its source.

The ordering of the Stream relies on the underlying collection just like an Iterator.

Streaming Files

The BufferedReader now has the lines() method which returns a Stream; for example[1]:

---

[1]Of course you should add a catch statement to this for error handling.

```
1  try (FileReader fr = new FileReader("file");
2      BufferedReader br = new BufferedReader(fr)) {
3      br.lines().forEach(System.out::println);
4  }
```

You can also read a file as a Stream using `Files.lines(Path filePath)`; for example:

```
1  try (Stream st = Files.lines(Paths.get("file"))) {
2      st.forEach(System.out::println);
3  }
```

Note this populates lazily; it does not read the entire file when you call it.

 Files.lines(Path): Any `IOException` that is thrown while processing the file (after the file is opened) will get wrapped in an `UncheckedIOException` and thrown.

Streaming File Trees

There are several static methods on the `Files` class for navigating file trees using a Stream.

- `list(Path dir)` – Stream of files in the given directory.
- `walk(Path dir)`[2] – Stream that traverses the file tree depth-first starting at the given directory.
- `walk(Path dir, int maxDepth)` – Same as walk(dir) but with a maximum depth.

Streaming Text Patterns

The Pattern[3] class now has a method, `splitAsStream(CharSequence)`, which creates a Stream.

For example:

```
1  import java.util.regex.Pattern;
2  // later on...
3  Pattern patt = Pattern.compile(",");
4  patt.splitAsStream("a,b,c")
5      .forEach(System.out::println);
```

The above uses a very simple pattern, a comma, and splits the text into a stream and prints it out. This would produce the following output:

---

[2]The actual method signature is `walk(Path start, FileVisitOption... options)` but you will probably just use `walk(Path)`.

[3]http://download.java.net/jdk8/docs/api/java/util/regex/Pattern.html

```
1   a
2   b
3   c
```

Infinite Streams

Using the generate or iterate static methods on Stream, you can create a Stream of values including never ending streams. For example, you could call generate in the following way to create an infinite supply of objects:

```
1   Stream.generate(() -> new Dragon());
```

For example, you could use this technique to produce a stream of CPU load or memory usage. However, you should use this with caution. It is similar to an infinite loop.

You could also use generate to create an infinite random number supply; for example:

```
1   Stream.generate(() -> Math.random());
```

However, the java.util.Random class does this for you with the following new methods: ints(), longs(), and doubles(). Each of those methods is overloaded with definitions similar to the following:

- ints(): An infinite Stream of random integers.
- ints(int n, int m): An infinite Stream of random integers from n (inclusive) to m (exclusive).
- ints(long size): A Stream of given size of random integers.
- ints(long size, int n, int m): A Stream of given size of random integers with given bounds.

The iterate method is similar to generate except it takes an initial value and a Function that modifies that value. For example, you can iterate over the Integers using the following code:

```
1   Stream.iterate(1, i -> i+1)
2       .forEach(System.out::print);
```

This would print out "1234…" continuously until you stop the program.

 There are ways to limit an infinite stream which we will cover later (filter and limit).

Ranges

There are also new methods for creating ranges of numbers as Streams.

For example, the static method, range, on the IntStream interface:

```
1   IntStream.range(1, 11)
2       .forEach(System.out::println);
```

The above would print out the numbers one through ten.

Each primitive Stream (IntStream, DoubleStream, and LongStream) has a corresponding `range` method.

Streaming Anything

You can create a Stream from any number of elements or an array using the two following methods:

```
1   Stream<Integer> s = Stream.of(1, 2, 3);
2   Stream<Object> s2 = Arrays.stream(array);
```

`Stream.of` can take any number of parameters of any type.

4.3 For Each

The most basic thing you can do with a Stream is loop through it using the `forEach` method.

For example, to print out all of the files in the current directory, you could do the following:

```
1   Files.list(Paths.get("."))
2       .forEach(System.out::println);
```

For the most part, this replaces the "for loop". It is more concise, and more object-oriented since you are delegating the implementation of the actual loop.

4.4 Map/Filter/Reduce

Lambda expressions and default methods allow us to implement map/filter/reduce in Java 8. Actually it is already implemented for us in the standard library.

For example, imagine you want to get the current point scores from a list of player-names and find the player with the most points. You have a simple class, `PlayerPoints`, and a `getPoints` method defined as the following:

```
1   public static class PlayerPoints {
2     public final String name;
3     public final long points;
4
5     public PlayerPoints(String name, long points) {
6       this.name = name;
7       this.points = points;
8     }
9
10    public String toString() {
11      return name + ":" + points;
12    }
13  }
14
15  public static long getPoints(final String name) {
16          // gets the Points for the Player
17  }
```

Finding the highest player could be done very simply in Java 8 as shown in the following code:

```
1   PlayerPoints highestPlayer =
2     names.stream().map(name -> new PlayerPoints(name, getPoints(name)))
3           .reduce(new PlayerPoints("", 0.0),
4                       (s1, s2) -> (s1.points > s2.points) ? s1 : s2);
```

This could also be done in Java 7 with the dollar library (or similarly with Guava or Functional-Java), but it would be much more verbose as shown in the following:

```
1   PlayerPoints highestPlayer =
2     $(names).map(new Function<String, PlayerPoints>() {
3                 public PlayerPoints call(String name) {
4                     return new PlayerPoints(name, getPoints(name));
5                 }
6         })
7           .reduce(new PlayerPoints("", 0.0),
8           new BiFunction<PlayerPoints, PlayerPoints, PlayerPoints>() {
9                 public PlayerPoints call(PlayerPoints s1, PlayerPoints s2) {
10                    return (s1.points > s2.points) ? s1 : s2;
11                }
12        });
```

The major benefit to coding this way (apart from the reduction in lines of code) is the ability to hide the underlying implementation of map/reduce. For example, it's possible that map and reduce are implemented concurrently, allowing you to easily take advantage of multiple processors. We'll describe one way to do this (ParallelArray) in the following section.

4.5 Parallel Array

The ParallelArray was part of JSR-166, but ended up being excluded from the standard Java lib[4]. It does exist and was released to the public domain (you can download it from the JSR website).

Although it was already out there, it really wasn't easy to use until closures were included in the Java language. In Java 7 using the ParallelArray looks like the following:

```
1    // with this class
2    public class Student {
3        String name;
4        int graduationYear;
5        double gpa;
6    }
7    // this predicate
8    final Ops.Predicate<Student> isSenior =
9            new Ops.Predicate<>() {
10                public boolean op(Student s) {
11                    return s.graduationYear == Student.THIS_YEAR;
12                }
13            };
14    // and this conversion operation
15    final Ops.ObjectToDouble<Student> selectGpa =
16            new Ops.ObjectToDouble<>() {
17                public double op(Student student) {
18                    return student.gpa;
19                }
20            };
21    // create a fork-join-pool
22    ForkJoinPool fjPool = new ForkJoinPool();
23    ParallelArray<Student> students = new ParallelArray<>(fjPool, data);
24    // find the best GPA:
25    double bestGpa = students.withFilter(isSenior)
26                             .withMapping(selectGpa)
27                             .max();
```

In Java 8, you can do the following:

---

[4]http://puredanger.com/tech/2009/11/15/jsr-166-concurrency-updates-hit-jdk-7/

```
1   // create a fork-join-pool
2   ForkJoinPool pool = new ForkJoinPool();
3   ParallelArray<Student> students = new ParallelArray<>(pool,data);
4   // find the best GPA:
5   double bestGpa = students
6       .withFilter((Student s) -> (s.graduationYear == THIS_YEAR))
7       .withMapping((Student s) -> s.gpa)
8       .max();
```

However, Java 8's addition of *stream()* and *parallelStream()* make this even easier:

```
1   double bestGpa = students
2       .parallelStream()
3       .filter(s -> (s.graduationYear == THIS_YEAR))
4       .mapToDouble(s -> s.gpa)
5       .max().getAsDouble();
```

This makes it extremely simple to switch between a sequential implementation and a concurrent one.

Groovy GPars

You can do something similar to this right now if you use Groovy with the GPars library in the following way:

```
1   GParsPool.withPool {
2       // a map-reduce functional style (students is a Collection)
3       def bestGpa = students.parallel
4           .filter{ s -> s.graduationYear == Student.THIS_YEAR }
5           .map{ s -> s.gpa }
6           .max()
7   }
```

The static method GParsPool.withPool takes in a closure and augments any Collection with several methods (using Groovy's Category mechanism). The parallel method actually creates a ParallelArray (JSR-166) from the given Collection and uses it with a thin wrapper around it.[a]

_____

[a] http://gpars.org/1.0.0/A>guide/guide/dataParallelism.html#dataParallelism_map-reduce

4.6 Peek

You can peek into a stream to do some action without interrupting the stream.

For example you could print out elements to debug code:

```
1  Files.list(Paths.get("."))
2      .map(Path::getFileName)
3      .peek(System.out::println)
4      .forEach(p -> doSomething(p));
```

You can use any action you want, but you should *not* try to modify elements; you should use map instead.

4.7 Limit

The limit(int n) method can be used to limit a stream to the given number of elements. For example:

```
1  Random rnd = new Random();
2  rnd.ints().limit(10)
3      .forEach(System.out::println);
```

The above would print out ten random integers.

4.8 Sort

Stream also has the sorted() method for sorting a stream. Like all *intermediate methods* on Stream (such as map, filter, and peek), the sorted() method executes lazily. Nothing happens until a terminating operation (such as reduce or forEach) is called. However, you should call a limiting operation like limit before calling sorted() on an infinite stream.

For example, the following would throw a runtime exception (using build 1.8.0-b132):

```
1  rnd.ints().sorted().limit(10)
2      .forEach(System.out::println);
```

However, the following code works just fine:

```
1  rnd.ints().limit(10).sorted()
2      .forEach(System.out::println);
```

If you have a finite stream, you can call `sorted()` before `filter` and know that Java will only sort what is necessary. For example, this code prints out the first five Java file-names in the current directory:

```
1  Files.list(Paths.get("."))
2      .map(Path::getFileName) // still a path
3      .map(Path::toString) // convert to Strings
4      .sorted() // sort them alphabetically
5      .filter(name -> name.endsWith(".java"))
6      .limit(5) // first 5
7      .forEach(System.out::println);
```

The code above does the following:

- Lists the files in the current directory.
- Maps those files to file names.
- Finds names that end with ".java".
- Takes only the first five (sorted alphabetically).
- Prints them out.

4.9 Collectors and Statistics

Since Streams are lazily evaluated and support parallel execution, you need a special way to combine results; this is called a *Collector*.

A *Collector* represents a way to combine the elements of a Stream into one result. It consists of three things:

- A *supplier* of an initial value.
- An *accumulator* which adds to the initial value.
- A *combiner* which combines two results into one.

There are two ways to do this: `collect(supplier,accumulator,combiner)`, or `collect(Collector)` (types left off for brevity).

Luckily, Java 8 comes with several Collectors built in. Import them the following way:

```
1   import static java.util.stream.Collectors.*;
```

Simple Collectors

The simplest collectors are things like toList() and toCollection():

```
1   // Accumulate names into a List
2   List<String> list = dragons.stream()
3           .map(Dragon::getName)
4           .collect(toList());
5
6   // Accumulate names into a TreeSet
7   Set<String> set = dragons.stream()
8           .map(Dragon::getName)
9           .collect(toCollection(TreeSet::new));
```

Joining

If you're familiar with Apache Commons' StringUtil.join, the joining collector is similar to it. It combines the stream using a given delimiter. For example:

```
1   String names = dragons.stream()
2           .map(Dragon::getName)
3           .collect(joining(","));
```

This would combine all of the names into one String separated by commas.

Statistics

More complex collectors resolve to a single value. For example, you can use an "averaging" Collector to get the average; for example:

```
1   System.out.println("\n----->Average line length:");
2   System.out.println(
3       Files.lines(Paths.get("Nio.java"))
4           .map(String::trim)
5           .filter(s -> !s.isEmpty())
6           .collect(averagingInt(String::length))
7           );
```

The above code calculates the average length of non-empty lines in the file "Nio.java".

Sometimes you want to collect multiple statistics about a collection. Because Streams are consumed when you call collect, you need to calculate all of your statistics at once. This is where *SummaryStatistics* comes in. First import the one you want to use:

```
1   import java.util.IntSummaryStatistics;
```

Then use the `summarizingInt` collector; for example:

```
1   IntSummaryStatistics stats = Files.lines(Paths.get("Nio.java"))
2           .map(String::trim)
3           .filter(s -> !s.isEmpty())
4           .collect(summarizingInt(String::length));
5
6   System.out.println(stats.getAverage());
7   System.out.println("count=" + stats.getCount());
8   System.out.println("max=" + stats.getMax());
9   System.out.println("min=" + stats.getMin());
```

The above code performs the same average as before, but also computes the maximum, minimum, and count of the elements.

 There's also `summarizingLong` and `summarizingDouble`.

Equivalently, you can map your stream to a primitive type and then call `summaryStatistics()`. For example:

```
1   IntSummaryStatistics stats = Files.lines(Paths.get("Nio.java"))
2       .map(String::trim)
3       .filter(s -> !s.isEmpty())
4       .mapToInt(String::length)
5       .summaryStatistics();
```

4.10 Grouping and Partitioning

The `groupingBy` collector groups elements based on a function you provide. For example:

```
1   // Group by first letter of name
2   List<Dragon> dragons = getDragons();
3   Map<Character,List<Dragon>> map = dragons.stream()
4           .collect(groupingBy(dragon -> dragon.getName().charAt(0)));
```

Similarly, the `partitioningBy` method creates a map with a boolean key. For example:

```
1   // Group by whether or not the dragon is green
2   Map<Boolean,List<Dragon>> map = dragons.stream()
3            .collect(partitioningBy(Dragon::isGreen));
```

 Parallel Grouping

To execute grouping in parallel (if you don't care about ordering) you should use the `groupingByConcurrent` method. The underlying stream should be unordered to allow grouping to occur in parallel; for example: `dragons.parallelStream().unordered().collect(groupingByConcurrent(Dragon::getColor));`.

4.11 Comparisons to Java 7

To better illustrate the benefit of Streams in Java 8, here are some examples of code from Java 7 compared to their new versions.

Finding a maximum

```
1   // Java 7
2   double max = 0;
3
4   for (Double d : list) {
5       if (d > max) {
6           max = d;
7       }
8   }
9   //Java 8
10  max = list.stream().reduce(0.0, Math::max);
11  // or
12  max = list.stream().mapToDouble(Number::doubleValue).max().getAsDouble();
```

Calculating an average

```
1  double total = 0;
2  double ave = 0;
3  // Java 7
4  for (Double d : list) {
5      total += d;
6  }
7  ave = total / ((double) list.size());
8  //Java 8
9  ave = list.stream().mapToDouble(Number::doubleValue).average().getAsDouble();
```

Printing the numbers one through ten

```
1  // Java 7
2  for (int i = 1; i < 11; i++) {
3      System.out.println(i);
4  }
5  // Java 8
6  IntStream.range(1, 11)
7      .forEach(System.out::println);
8  //or
9  Stream.iterate(1, i -> i+1).limit(10)
10     .forEach(System.out::println);
```

Joining Strings

```
1  // Java 7 using commons-util
2  List<String> names = new LinkedList<>();
3  for (Dragon dragon : dragons)
4      names.add(dragon.getName());
5  String names = StringUtils.join(names, ",");
6  // Java 8
7  String names = dragons.stream()
8      .map(Dragon::getName)
9      .collect(Collectors.joining(","));
```

5 Optional

Java 8 comes with the `Optional` class in the `java.util` package for avoiding null return values (and thus `NullPointerException`). It is very similar to Google Guava's Optional[1], which is similar to Nat Pryce's Maybe[2] class and Scala's `Option` class.

The Billion Dollar Mistake

Tony Hoare, the inventor of null, has gone on record calling it his "billion-dollar mistake"[a]. Despite your opinion of null, many efforts have been made to make null-checks part of the compilation or automated-code-check process; for example, the @Nonnull annotation of JSR-305. `Optional` makes it very simple for API designers to avoid null.

———————
[a]http://qconlondon.com/london-2009/presentation/Null+References:+The+Billion+Dollar+Mistake

---

You can use `Optional.of(x)` to wrap a non-null value, `Optional.empty()` to represent a missing value, or `Optional.ofNullable(x)` to create an Optional from a reference that may or may not be null.

After creating an instance of Optional, you then use `isPresent()` to determine if the there is a value and `get()` to get the value. Optional provides a few other helpful methods for dealing with missing values:

- `orElse(T)` – Returns the given default value if the Optional is empty.
- `orElseGet(Supplier<T>)` – Calls on the given Supplier to provide a value if the Optional is empty.
- `orElseThrow(Supplier<X extends Throwable>)` – Calls on the given Supplier for an exception to throw if the Optional is empty.

It also includes functional style (lambda friendly) methods, like the following:

- `filter(Predicate<? super T> predicate)` – Filters the value and returns a new Optional.
- `flatMap(Function<? super T,Optional<U>> mapper)` – Performs a mapping operation which returns an Optional.

———————
[1]http://docs.guava-libraries.googlecode.com/git/javadoc/com/google/common/base/Optional.html
[2]http://www.natpryce.com/articles/000776.html

- `ifPresent(Consumer<? super T> consumer)` – Executes the given Consumer only if there is a value present (no return value).
- `map(Function<? super T,? extends U> mapper)` – Uses the given mapping Function and returns a new Optional.

Stream Optional

The new `Stream` interface has multiple methods which return Optional (in case there are no values in the Stream):

- `reduce(BinaryOperator<T> accumulator)` – Reduces the stream to a single value.
- `max(Comparator<? super T> comparator)` – Finds the maximum value.
- `min(Comparator<? super T> comparator)` – Finds the minimum value.

6 Nashorn

Nashorn replaces Rhino as the default JavaScript engine for the Oracle JVM. Nashorn is much faster since it uses the `invokedynamic` feature of the JVM. It also includes a command line tool (`jjs`).

6.1 jjs

JDK 8 includes the command line tool `jjs` for running JavaScript.

You can run JavaScript files from the command line (assuming you have Java 8's bin in your PATH):

```
1  $ jjs script.js
```

This can be useful for running scripts; for example, let's say you wanted to quickly find the sum of some numbers:

```
1  var data = [1, 3, 5, 7, 11]
2  var sum = data.reduce(function(x, y) {return x + y}, 0)
3  print(sum)
```

Running the above code should print out 27.

6.2 Scripting

Running jjs with the `-scripting` option starts up an interactive shell where you can type and evaluate JavaScript.

You can also embed variables into strings and have them evaluate; for example:

```
1  jjs> var date = new Date()
2  jjs> print("${date}")
```

This would print out the current date and time.

6.3 ScriptEngine

You can also run JavaScript dynamically from Java.

First, you need to import the ScriptEngine:

```
1  import javax.script.ScriptEngine;
2  import javax.script.ScriptEngineManager;
```

Second, you use the `ScriptEngineManager` to get the Nashorn engine:

```
1  ScriptEngineManager engineManager = new ScriptEngineManager();
2  ScriptEngine engine = engineManager.getEngineByName("nashorn");
```

Now you can evaluate javascript at any point:

```
1  engine.eval("function p(s) { print(s) }");
2  engine.eval("p('Hello Nashorn');");
```

The `eval` method can also take a `FileReader` as input:

```
1  engine.eval(new FileReader('library.js'));
```

This way you can include and run any JavaScript. However, keep in mind that the typical variables available to you in the browser (window, document, etc.) are not available.

6.4 Importing

You can import and use Java classes and packages using the *JavaImporter*.

For example, import `java.util`, the IO, and NIO file packages:

```
1  var imports = new JavaImporter(java.util, java.io, java.nio.file);
2  with (imports) {
3          var paths = new LinkedList();
4          print(paths instanceof LinkedList); //true
5          paths.add(Paths.get("file1"));
6          paths.add(Paths.get("file2"));
7          paths.add(Paths.get("file3"));
8          print(paths) // [file1, file2, file3]
9  }
```

The above demonstrates that `paths` is an instance of `LinkedList` and prints out the list.

Later on you could add the following code to write text into the files:

```
1  for (var i=0; i < paths.size(); i++)
2          Files.newOutputStream(paths.get(i))
3                    .write("test\n".getBytes());
```

We can use existing Java classes, but we can also create new ones.

6.5 Extending

You can extend Java classes and interfaces using the Java.type and Java.extend functions. For example, you can extend the Callable interface and implement the call method:

```
1  var concurrent = new JavaImporter(java.util, java.util.concurrent);
2  var Callable = Java.type("java.util.concurrent.Callable");
3  with (concurrent) {
4    var executor = Executors.newCachedThreadPool();
5    var tasks = new LinkedHashSet();
6    for (var i=0; i < 200; i++) {
7      var MyTask = Java.extend(Callable, {call: function() {print("task " + i)}})
8      var task = new MyTask();
9      tasks.add(task);
10     executor.submit(task);
11   }
12 }
```

6.6 Invocable

You can also invoke JavaScript functions directly from Java.

Firstly, you need to cast the engine to the Invocable interface:

```
1  Invocable inv = (Invocable) engine;
```

Then, to invoke any function, simple use the invokeFunction method, for example:

```
1  engine.eval("function p(s) { print(s) }");
2  inv.invokeFunction("p", "hello");
```

Lastly, you can use the getInterface method to implement any interface in JavaScript.

For example, if you have the following JPrinter interface, you can use it like so:

```
1  public static interface JPrinter {
2      void p(String s);
3  }
4  // later on...
5  JPrinter printer = inv.getInterface(JPrinter.class);
6  printer.p("Hello again!");
```

7 New Date and Time API

Java 8 introduces a new Date/Time API that is thread-safe, easier to read, and more comprehensive than the previous API. Java's Calendar implementation has not changed much since it was first introduced and Joda-Time[1] is widely regarded as a better replacement. Java 8's new Date/Time API is very similar to Joda-Time.

7.1 New Classes

The main difference you will notice is that there are several different classes to represent time, date, time period, and timezone specific data. Also there are transformers for dates and times.

For dates and times without a timezone, use the following:

- LocalDate – Day, month, year.
- LocalTime – Time of day only.
- LocalDateTime – Both date and time.

For timezone specific times you use ZonedDateTime.

Previous to Java 8, to calculate the time eight hours in the future you would need to write something like the following:

```
1  Calendar cal = Calendar.getInstance();
2  cal.add(Calendar.HOUR, 8);
3  cal.getTime(); // actually returns a Date
```

In Java 8, you can more simply write the following:

```
1  LocalTime now = LocalTime.now();
2  LocalTime later = now.plus(8, HOURS);
```

There are also well-named methods such as plusDays, plusMonths, minusDays, and minusMonths. For example:

---

[1]http://www.joda.org/joda-time/

```
1   LocalDate today = LocalDate.now();
2   LocalDate thirtyDaysFromNow = today.plusDays(30);
3   LocalDate nextMonth = today.plusMonths(1);
4   LocalDate aMonthAgo = today.minusMonths(1);
```

Note that each method returns a different instance of LocalDate. The original LocalDate, today, remains unchanged. This is because the new Date-Time types are immutable. This allows them to be thread-safe and cacheable.

7.2 Creation

Creating new date and time objects is much easier and less error-prone in Java 8. Every type is immutable and has static factory methods.

For example, creating a new LocalDate for March 15, 2014 is as simple as:

```
1   LocalDate date = LocalDate.of(2014, 3, 15);
```

For more type-safety, you can use the new Month enum:

```
1   date = LocalDate.of(2014, Month.MARCH, 15);
```

You can also easily create a LocalDateTime by combining an instance of LocalDate with a LocalTime:

```
1   LocalTime time = LocalTime.of(12, 15, 0);
2   LocalDateTime datetime = date.atTime(time);
```

You could also use any of the following methods (on LocalDate):

- atTime(int hour, int minute)
- atTime(int hour, int minute, int second)
- atTime(int hour, int minute, int second, int nanoOfSecond)

Every class also has the now() method, which corresponds to the instant (or date) it is called.

7.3 Enums

Java 8 adds several enums, such as java.time.temporal.ChronoUnit for expressing things like "days" and "hours" instead of the integer constants used in the Calendar API. For example:

```
1  LocalDate today = LocalDate.now();
2  LocalDate nextWeek = today.plus(1, ChronoUnit.WEEKS);
3  LocalDate nextMonth = today.plus(1, ChronoUnit.MONTHS);
4  LocalDate nextYear = today.plus(1, ChronoUnit.YEARS);
5  LocalDate nextDecade = today.plus(1, ChronoUnit.DECADES);
```

There's also the `java.time.DayOfWeek` and `java.time.Month` enums.

The month enum can be used to create LocalDates and is returned by `LocalDate::getMonth`. For example here is how you might create a LocalDate and print out the month.

```
1  // import java.time.Month;
2  LocalDate date = LocalDate.of(2014, Month.MARCH, 27);
3  System.out.println(date.getMonth());
```

This would print out "MARCH".

7.4 Clock

The `Clock` can be used in conjunction with dates and times to help build your tests. During production a normal Clock can be used, and a different one during tests.

To get the default clock, use the following:

```
1  Clock.systemDefaultZone();
```

The Clock can then be passed into factory methods; for example:

```
1  LocalTime time = LocalTime.now(clock);
```

7.5 Period and Duration

Java 8 has two types for representing time differences as humans understand them, Period and Duration.

Duration is a time-based amount of time, such as '34.5 seconds'. Period is a date-based amount of time, such as '2 years, 3 months and 4 days'.

Periods and Durations can be determined using the `between` method:

```
1  Period p = Period.between(date1, date2);
2  Duration d = Duration.between(time1, time2);
```

They can also be created using static methods. For example, Durations can be created for any amount of seconds, minutes, hours, or days:

```
1  Duration twoHours = Duration.ofHours(2);
2  Duration tenMinutes = Duration.ofMinutes(10);
3  Duration thirtySecs = Duration.ofSeconds(30);
```

Periods and Durations can be added or subtracted from Java 8 date types. For example:

```
1  LocalTime t2 = time.plus(twoHours);
```

7.6 Temporal Adjusters

A `TemporalAdjuster` can be used to do tricky date "math" that is popular in business applications. For example they can be used to find the "first Monday of the month" or "next Tuesday".

The `java.time.temporal.TemporalAdjusters` class contains a bunch of useful methods for creating TemporalAdjusters. Here are a few of them:

- firstDayOfMonth()
- firstDayOfNextMonth()
- firstInMonth(DayOfWeek)
- lastDayOfMont()
- next(DayOfWeek)
- nextOrSame(DayOfWeek)
- previous(DayOfWeek)
- previousOrSame(DayOfWeek)

To use a `TemporalAdjuster` use the `with` method. This method returns an adjusted copy of the date-time or date object. For example:

```
1  import static java.time.temporal.TemporalAdjusters.*;
2  //...
3  LocalDate nextTuesday = LocalDate.now().with(next(DayOfWeek.TUESDAY));
```

7.7 Instant

The Instant class represents a point in time measured to the nanosecond. It forms the basis of time measurements in the Java 8 date-time API.

Much like the old Date class, Instant measures time starting from the "epoch" (Jan. 1, 1970) and is time-zone ignorant.

7.8 Time Zones

Time-Zones are represented by the java.time.ZoneId class. There are two types of ZoneIds, fixed offsets and geographical regions. This is to compensate for things like "daylight saving time" which can be very complex.

You can get an instance of a ZoneId in many ways including the following two:

```
ZoneId mountainTime = ZoneId.of("America/Denver");
ZoneId myZone = ZoneId.systemDefault();
```

To print out all available IDs, use getAvailableZoneIds():

```
System.out.println(ZoneId.getAvailableZoneIds());
```

7.9 Backwards Compatibility

The original Date and Calendar objects have the toInstant() method to convert them to the new Date-Time API. You can then use an ofInstant(Insant,ZoneId) method to get a LocalDateTime or ZonedDateTime object; for example:

```
Date date = new Date();
Instant now = date.toInstant();
LocalDateTime dateTime = LocalDateTime.ofInstant(now, myZone);
ZonedDateTime zdt = ZonedDateTime.ofInstant(now, myZone);
```

8 No More Permanent Generation

The proposed implementation will allocate class meta-data in native memory and move interned Strings and class statics to the Java heap. [http://openjdk.java.net/jeps/122]

Most allocations for the class metadata are now allocated out of native memory. This means that you won't have to set the "XX:PermSize" options anymore (they don't exist).

This also means that you will get a "java.lang.OutOfMemoryError: Metadata space" error message instead of "java.lang.OutOfMemoryError: Permgen space" when you run out of memory.

This is part of the convergence of the Oracle JRockit and HotSpot JVMs.

9 Miscellaneous

Java 8 has tons of new features that you might miss with all of the focus on lambdas. Here are some of them:

- java.util.Base64
- Cryptography upgrades (lots)
- JDBC 4.2
- Repeatable Annotations
- Annotations on types

For a more complete list, please see the official list[1].

9.1 Base64

Until now, Java developers have had to rely on third-party libraries for encoding and decoding Base-64. Since it is such a frequent operation, a large project will typically contain several different implementations of Base64. For example: Apache commons-codec, Spring, and Guava all have separate implementations.

For this reason, Java 8 has `java.util.Base64`. It acts like a factory for Base64 encoders and decoders and has the following methods:

- `getEncoder()`
- `getDecoder()`
- `getUrlEncoder()`
- `getUrlDecoder()`

Each factory method returns either an Encoder or Decoder.

The URL Base-64 Encoder provides an encoding that is URL and Filename safe (62 is - and 63 is _).

9.2 Annotations on Java Types

Prior to Java 8, annotations could be used on any declaration. In Java 8, annotations can also be applied to the *use of types*. Here are some examples:

---

[1]http://openjdk.java.net/projects/jdk8/features/

```
1   // Class instance creation:
2   new @Interned RocketShip();
3
4   // Type cast:
5   notNullString = (@NonNull String) str;
6
7   // implements clause:
8   class ImmutableSet<T> implements
9           @Readonly Set<@Readonly T> { ... }
10
11  // Thrown exception declaration:
12  void launchRocket() throws
13              @Critical FireException { ... }
```

This new ability is primarily aimed at supporting type-checking frameworks, such as Checker[2]. These frameworks help find errors in your code at compile time.

9.3 Repeating Annotations

Java 8 will allow annotations annotated with @Repeatable to be repeated.

For example, let's say you're coding a game and want to use annotations to schedule when methods should be called. You can declare multiple schedules using multiple annotations:

```
1   // the first of the month and every monday at 7am
2   @Schedule(dayOfMonth="first")
3   @Schedule(dayOfWeek="Monday", hour=7)
4   public void doGoblinInvasion() { ... }
```

For this to be possible, you need to have the following:

- The Schedule annotation needs to use the meta-annotation @Repeatable.
- There needs to be another annotation as declared by the @Repeatable annotation.

Due to Java's emphasis on backwards-compatibility, repeating annotations are actually stored within another annotation (that you provide). The @Repeatable annotation takes in a value that is the class of the containing annotation. For example:

---

[2]http://types.cs.washington.edu/checker-framework/

```
1  // Schedule.java
2  @Repeatable(Schedules.class)
3  public @interface Schedule {...}
4  // Schedules.java
5  public @interface Schedules {
6      Schedule[] value;
7  }
```

Schedule is now a *repeatable annotation.*

You can use reflection to access repeatable annotations at runtime. To do this there is a new method called getAnnotationsByType(Class annotationClass) on Class, Constructor, Method, etc. It returns an array of all such annotations (or an empty array if there are none).

10 Functional Programming in Java 8

Java 8 manages to add many of the features of functional languages without significantly changing the Java language.

When lambda expressions, method-references, the Stream interface, and immutable data-structures are combined, Java enables what could be called "functional programming" (FP).

For the purposes of this book, the three pillars of FP are as follows:

- Functions
- Immutability
- Concurrency

10.1 Functions

Of course, as the name implies, functional programming is based on functions as a first-class feature. Java 8 arguably elevates functions to a first-class feature with the Lambda Project and *functional interfaces*.

The `Function` interface (and related interfaces IntFunction, DoubleFunction, LongFunction, BiFunction, etc.) represents the compromise made by Java 8 in elevating functions to objects. This interface allows functions to be passed as arguments, stored as variables, and be returned by methods.

The `Function` interface has the following default methods:

- `andThen(Function)`: Returns a composed function that first applies this function to its input, and then applies the given function to the result.
- `compose(Function)`: Similar to `andThen` but in reversed order (first applies the given function to its input, and then this function).
- `identity()`: Returns a function that always returns its input argument.

You can use these methods to create a chain for creating a function; for example:

```
1  Function<Integer,String> f = Function.<Integer>identity()
2          .andThen(i -> 2*i).andThen(i -> "str" + i);
```

The resulting function would take an Integer, multiply it by two, and then prepend "str" to it.

You can use `andThen` any number of times to create a single function. Also, remember that functions can be passed and returned from methods. Here's an example involving the new Date-Time API:

```
1   public Function<LocalDate,LocalDateTime> dateTimeFunction(
2       final Function<LocalDate,LocalDate> f) {
3
4       return f.andThen(d -> d.atTime(2, 2));
5   }
```

This method would take in a function that operates on a LocalDate and convert it into a function that returns a LocalDateTime (with a time of 2:02am).

Tuples

If you need a functional interface for a method with more than two parameters (eg. "TriFunction") you need to make it yourself or use a library. Another way to handle this issue is to use a data structure called a *Tuple*.

A Tuple is a typed data structure for holding a number of elements. Some languages, such as Scala, have built-in support for Tuples. Tuples are useful whenever you are handling multiple related values, but don't want all of the overhead of creating a new class.

Here's a very simple example of implementing a Tuple with two elements:

```
1   public class Tuple2<A, B> {
2       public final A _1;
3       public final B _2;
4
5       public Tuple2(A a, B b) {
6               this._1 = a;
7               this._2 = b;
8       }
9
10      @Override
11      public A get_1() {
12              return _1;
13      }
14
15      @Override
16      public B get_2() {
17              return _2;
18      }
19  }
```

Tuples also allow you to approximate returning multiple values.

There are several implementations of Tuples available in Java, such as javatuples[1] and totallylazy[2].

10.2 Immutability

In functional programming, state is considered harmful and avoided whenever possible. Instead, *immutable* (unchangeable) data structures are preferred. For example, String is an immutable type in Java.

As you may have learned, Java 8's new Date-Time classes are immutable. What you may not have realized is that *almost everything* added in Java 8 is immutable (Optional and Streams for example).

However, you need to be careful when using Java 8's new functional patterns to not accidentally fall back into the *mutable* mind-set. For example, the following type of code should be avoided:

```
int[] myCount = new int[1];
list.forEach(dragon -> {
    if (dragon.isGreen()) myCount[0]++;
}
```

You may think you are being clever, but this kind of thing can cause problems. Instead, you should do something like the following:

```
list.stream().filter(Dragon::isGreen).count();
```

If you ever find yourself resorting to mutability, consider if you could use some combination of "filter", "map", "reduce" or "collect" instead.

10.3 Concurrency

With the increasing popularity of multi-core processors, concurrent programming has become more important. Functional programming forms a solid basis for concurrent programming and Java 8 supports concurrency in many different ways.

One of those ways is the parallelStream() method on Collection. It provides a very quick way to use a Stream concurrently. However, like all optimizations, you should test to make sure that your code is actually faster, and it should be used sparingly. Too much concurrency could actually cause your application to slow down.

---

[1]http://www.javatuples.org/

[2]https://code.google.com/p/totallylazy/

Another way Java 8 supports concurrency is with the new CompletableFuture class. It has the supplyAsync static method that takes in the functional interface Supplier. It also has the method thenAccept which takes in a Consumer that handles completion of the task. The CompletableFuture calls on the given supplier in a different thread and executes the consumer when complete.

When used in conjunction with things like the CountDownLatch, AtomicInteger, AtomicLong, AtomicReference, ... you can implement thread-safe, concurrent FP-like code; for example:

```java
public Dragon closestDragon(Location location) {
    AtomicReference<DragonDistance> closest =
        new AtomicReference<>(DragonDistance.worstMatch());
    CountDownLatch latch = new CountDownLatch(dragons.size());
    dragons.forEach(dragon -> {
        CompletableFuture.supplyAsync(() -> dragon.distance(location))
            .thenAccept(result -> {
              closest.accumulateAndGet(result, DragonDistance::closest);
              latch.countDown();
              });
        });
    try {
        latch.await();
    } catch (InterruptedException e) {
        throw new RuntimeException("Interrupted during calculations", e);
    }
    return closest.get().getDragon();
}
```

This example finds the closest dragon to a certain Location (assume that Dragon's distance method involves a time-consuming calculation).

However, this could be simplified using the parallelStream() default method (since only one type of calculation is going on) in the following way:

```java
public Dragon closestDragon(Location location) {
    return dragons.parallelStream()
        .map(dragon -> dragon.distance(location))
        .reduce(DistancePair.worstMatch(), DragonDistance::closest)
        .getDragon();
}
```

This performs essentially the same task as the previous example but in a more concise (and functional) way.

10.4 Tail-Call Optimization

One of the hallmarks of functional programming is *tail-call recursion*[3]. It solves the same problem as iteration (which does not exist in FP). Unfortunately, it can cause stack-overflows if not properly optimized by the compiler.

Tail-Call optimization refers to when a compiler converts a recursive function call into a loop to avoid using the call stack. For example, a function that uses tail-call recursion in Lisp will be automatically optimized this way.

Java 8 does not support tail-call optimization like some other languages (yet). However, it is possible to approximate it using something like the following interface:

```java
@FunctionalInterface
public interface Tail<T> {

    Tail<T> apply();

    default boolean isDone() {
        return false;
    }

    default T result() {
        throw new UnsupportedOperationException("Not done yet.");
    }

    default T invoke() {
        return Stream.iterate(this, Tail::apply)
                .filter(Tail::isDone)
                .findFirst()
                .get()
                .result();
    }
}
```

The `Tail` interface has three default methods and one abstract-method (apply). The `invoke()` method contains the meat of the "tail-call optimization":

- It takes advantage of Stream's `iterate` method to create an infinite Stream which will continuously call Tail's `apply` method.
- Then it uses `filter` and `findFirst` to stop the Stream when `isDone()` returns true.
- Finally, it returns the result.

To implement the "done" condition, there is the following additional static method on Tail:

---

[3]Tail call recursion is when a function call happens inside a function as its final action.

```
1  static <T> Tail<T> done(final T value) {
2      return new Tail<T>() {
3          @Override
4          public T result() {
5            return value;
6          }
7          @Override
8          public boolean isDone() {
9            return true;
10          }
11          @Override
12          public Tail<T> apply() {
13            throw new UnsupportedOperationException("Not supported.");
14          }
15      };
16  }
```

With the Tail interface you can mimic tail-call recursion quite easily in Java 8. Here's an example of calculating *factorial* using this interface:

```
1  public static Long fastFactorial(int n) {
2      return fastFactorial(1L, n).invoke();
3  }
4  private static Tail<Long> fastFactorial(long x, int n) {
5      return () -> {
6          switch (n) {
7              case 1:
8                  return Tail.done(x);
9              default:
10                  return fastFactorial(x * n, n - 1);
11          }
12      };
13  }
```

Using this method, you can make extremely fast programs while still maintaining the functional style.

Of course the JVM does a lot optimization by itself, so this may not always be the best course. However, it is something to keep in mind.

11 Conclusion

Thank you for reading this short introduction to Java 8. Hopefully you learned a lot and are ready to starting using it yourself.

To recap, Java 8 includes the following:

- Lambda expressions
- Method references
- Default Methods (Defender methods)
- A new Stream API.
- Optional
- A new Date/Time API.
- Nashorn, the new JavaScript engine
- Removal of the Permanent Generation

To keep track of possible future features of Java, you might want to look at JEPS[1].

---

[1]http://openjdk.java.net/jeps/0

Backports

If for some reason you can't immediately upgrade to Java 8, there are some ways to backport some Java 8 features to previous versions.

For each of the following features, here is the backport or similar library:

- Lambdas – Retrolambda[2]
- Lazily Evaluated Sequences – totallylazy[3]
- Optional – guava[4]
- Date/Time – ThreeTen[5]
- Nashorn – nashorn-backport[6]

Use the backports with caution.

[2]https://github.com/orfjackal/retrolambda
[3]https://code.google.com/p/totallylazy/
[4]https://code.google.com/p/guava-libraries/
[5]http://www.threeten.org/
[6]https://bitbucket.org/ramonza/nashorn-backport